Front cover image: **Amelia Scimone** | Micaela Scimone

First published in Great Britain in 2011.

Publisher | Facing It Publications
32a Bisham Gardens
London N6 6DD

Graphic Design | Lauren T Franks
www.lauren-t-franks.com

Printers | Book Binders of London
www.bookbindersoflondon.com

ISBN 978-0-9566497-1-3

Facing It

Reflections on Images of Older Women

by Harriet Walter

Edited by Joan Scanlon

Facing It Publications

So much has been said and sung of beautiful young girls,
why doesn't somebody wake up to the beauty of old women?

Harriet Beecher Stowe, Uncle Tom's Cabin

Opposite: **Mary Vivian** | Boo Beaumont

Preface & Acknowledgements

Young girls and women are conditioned to aspire to look like other people. From an early age, we leaf through magazines measuring ourselves up against airbrushed images of a fairly narrow standard of female perfection. In my teens during the 60s, photographs of Twiggy and Jean Shrimpton, Françoise Hardy and Jane Asher filled the pages of the glossy mags. These icons did their work of imprinting an aspiration on my young impressionable mind, and creating a yardstick by which to judge my own image. This was the power of photography.

The habit of aspiration dies hard and as I hit my fifties I wanted some role models to help me move into the next stage of life. I could find few if any photographic images of women my age to emulate. There were plenty of images of youthful perfection but I didn't want to be young any more. I wanted to be the age I am.

I approached a photographer friend of mine, Jill Kennington – herself one of the top models of the 60s and who has taken age in her unartificial stride – with a view to creating an exhibition celebrating the beauty of older women. Jill produced some terrific portraits she had already taken, but it wasn't until I teamed up with the RSC while playing Cleopatra – a woman of reputedly irresistible charms but who expresses great insecurity about her own ageing that I could commission Jill to take more photographs. Alexandra Myers then came on board to do some picture research, and the rest of the photographs were collected from friends, friends of friends, strangers in the street, and from the various photographers themselves.

In the exhibition I deliberately juxtaposed the famous with the non-famous, the 50 year olds with the 90 year olds. We are all in this together. I have expanded the collection for this book and, by encouraging people to look quietly at such a range of photographs, I hope to re-adjust our focus a bit, to look beyond the surface and see the infinite variety of ways in which a woman can captivate our attention and more importantly, enjoy living in her own skin.

The exhibition has now been shown at a number of different venues and events, and I am grateful to all the individuals who enabled the exhibition to be restaged in recent years: The Royal Shakespeare Theatre, Stratford-upon-Avon (2006); The Capital Arts Centre, Warwick University (2007); the Cheltenham Literary Festival (2008); the Stratford Literary Festival (2008); The Sturminster Newton Festival (2009); the Salisbury Arts Centre (2010); the Smith and Williamson offices in Salisbury (2010) and the National Theatre, Olivier Theatre Foyer (2010). In the coming year, I am delighted that a smaller version of the exhibition is going to be restaged at various venues around the UK by the magazine Woman's Weekly, as part of their centenary celebrations, and I am grateful to the editor, Diane Kenwood, for making these images available to a wider audience.

I have had so much practical help and encouragement in developing this collection of photographs that I will just have to list names: Faith Evans, my literary agent; Gregory Doran, for connecting me to David Howells at the RSC who put on the original exhibition in Stratford in 2006 and who continues to help; Susie Sainsbury and Damon de Laszlo, who helped financially; Alexandra Myers for her expertise and picture research; my cousin, Veronica Stewart, who led me to the Salisbury Arts Centre team headed by Judy Adam; Carinthia West for giving me encouragement and introductions; Eileen Hogan for helping me arrange a website; Cathy Courtenay for curatorial help; Alison Chown and her team for coordinating the exhibition at the National Theatre, and the NT press office; Romley Davies publicists for their support and hard work in getting the word out.

I had always dreamed of making the collection into a book but it proved hard to get commercial publishers to take the project on. All this seemed to confirm the prejudices in the market place despite the fact that so many members of the public who saw the exhibition commented that it should be turned into a book. It is thanks to my friend and editor Joan Scanlon, who wholeheartedly took up the cause, that we have managed to produce this book ourselves. Joan gave me vital practical help as well as immeasurably valuable encouragement. Thanks to Lauren T Franks for her speediness, expertise and creativity in the design and production first of a catalogue for the NT show and now this book. It is particularly due to Joan and Lauren working to an almost impossible deadline that this book has become a reality.

I am grateful to all of those who have allowed us to reproduce the images and extracts from literary texts represented in this book. Thanks to Mark McCloud at Curtis Brown for obtaining permission to use *Someone to Wave Goodbye* by S.E. Hinton; to Alan Brodie for obtaining permission to reproduce lyrics from *I've Been To A Marvellous Party* by Nöel Coward; and to Farrar, Straus and Giroux for permission to reprint an extract from the poem *One Art* by Elizabeth Bishop. Thanks also to Dianne Butterworth for proof-reading the final text, and to Maya T Franks for moral, artistic and technical support. I thank all the photographers for letting me take advantage of their individual vision and talent, and for permission to reproduce their photographs. Special thanks to the prolific Jill Kennington, and to Georgia Oetker, Sophie Lambe, Garlinda Birkbeck, Katrin Talbot and Simon Annand who have been particularly generous throughout the development of this project.

Last but not least I would like to thank the bravery of the sitters, many of whom are not used to public scrutiny.

Harriet Walter
London, 2011

Introduction

by Harriet Walter

The photographic image is the most easily transmittable comment about ourselves that we can make. It leaps over language barriers and national boundaries, can be reproduced in seconds and simultaneously viewed in magazines, newspapers, and in multiple forms on the internet. It can also be slowly gazed at in a gallery or room.

Because it is such an easy currency to exchange, the outward appearance of a complex human being is the one that reaches us most immediately and can be exploited to prejudice our judgments of the inner person. In the Infinite Variety exhibition, and in the images in this book, the sitters look out at us from their frames defying the prejudice that tells us they are no longer interesting or valuable or beautiful.

One of the many things that prompted the idea for the exhibition was hearing so many women complain that over a certain age they became invisible. A collection of photographs seemed a very simple and direct way of starting to redress the balance, and flout that invisibility.

In our society, signs of encroaching age are loathed as reminders of a process of ultimate decay, so we are encouraged to freeze time through surgery and botox. We nip and tuck and waste precious time, obsessed with an ultimately hopeless mission. We can still look great, but should we be trying to look young? Why not celebrate the gains in depth, personality and individuality that we have traded for the flawless glow of youth? Why not learn to love grey and silver and delicately etched lines, even saggy pouches? Why not embrace the transitions, the contradictions and storylines layered into a lived-in face?

My initial quest for role models was about how to look good as one got older, but it soon became clear that women growing older become less vain and that one of the advantages of being largely ignored by the fashion market is that we can develop our own style, or lack of it. We can make our own rules.

This goes for the inner 'rules' as well. We can decide how we want to live the rest of our lives, based on increased self-knowledge and influenced by the wisdom and guidelines of other women who have been there before us. In developing the exhibition into a book I have interwoven written passages of my own observations and attempts to come to terms with my own ageing, together with quotes from others, from literary texts and interviews.

I discuss some of the particular problems for older women in the acting profession, but I am also simply a woman growing older, and as such I am concerned to find and celebrate all the positive qualities that women acquire with age: wisdom, mellowness, humour, daring, a certain 'alternative' outlook, an acerbity, a sense of irony, impatience with fools, directness, so many things. In my view, these newly acquired qualities grow alongside a different kind of beauty.

I was amazed at and grateful for the enthusiasm and generosity of the sitters for the Infinite Variety exhibition. With very few exceptions women were happy to be photographed or to lend photos which showed their present faces in an honest way. I observed that it was easier for those over 75. Those women who had passed beyond that indeterminate 'middle age' and definitely owned up to the description 'old' were proud to be old. They were philosophical about it, amused by or indifferent to the idea of their faces being scrutinised in a photograph. Women in the much looser category of the middle-aged had more varied reactions.

It has a lot to do with the fact that deep down in our culture, we have linked physical beauty with sexual desirability, and since conventional beauty is associated with youth in the popular imagination, we allow ourselves to believe that at a certain age a woman stops being sexually desirable. The trouble is that, unless we are in a happy sexual relationship in our middle and old age, we tend to internalise these ideas. We stop feeling desirable even if we don't relinquish our own desires. We feel vulnerable being looked at too closely because we are no longer at our 'best', because 'best' is synonymous with our younger selves.

Some of the middle-aged sitters had never considered themselves conventionally beautiful and were flattered to find themselves thought so now. Others had been acknowledged beauties in their youth and out of a wide choice of flattering photos they could have submitted, actually chose to send in the picture which showed them without make-up or soft lighting, toothy, fleshy and fabulously real. Perhaps their earlier confidence in their looks was a life-long gift. Perhaps they were relieved of the pressure of looking perfect and were celebrating their new-found liberation.

In gathering this collection I encountered many paradoxes. Some of the well-known faces responded positively in person – but then I would be sent a very air-brushed, glammed-up publicity photo from a protective agent. Many women in their 50s just didn't look old enough to be in a book about ageing, which of course was one of the points I wanted to make but a hard one to demonstrate in a photograph. I set an arbitrary lower age limit of late forties. The upper end was limitless and the oldest sitter in the book is 99 at the time of writing.

For the last 8 years or so I have been continuously absorbed by this idea and see potential subjects for portraits on every tube ride I take. I also find so many of my friends beautiful but, as most of my friends are actors and I wanted to spread the collection more widely, I have ended up almost eliminating my actor friends for which I apologise.

I started the collection in a rather random way, approaching friends and acquaintances. As I extended the collection, I wanted the term 'Infinite Variety' to be meaningful, across race and class, and have sought new

13

subjects from my own immediate world, and from amongst the beautiful women I see everyday on the tube, and in the supermarket. It is an alarming thing to approach total strangers in the street, and no doubt alarming for them too! Where this has created a positive connection it has been extremely rewarding and produced great results, and I am gradually getting over my cowardice as I continue to extend the collection for a website.

A photographic portrait is a paradox. It is a two-dimensional surface (literally skin deep) from which the viewer infers a three-dimensional depth, a depth which none but the owner of the face can truly reach or feel. Looking at an-other person's face quietly and privately pricks our empathetic imagination as we try to get behind the eyes.

As an actor – and simply out of curiosity about other people – I am interested in the inside behind the outside skin that we can see. The older the person, the longer the story, and the harder to sum up accurately in a package. In the commercial world it is the opposite; the surface perfection of youth is something we can project any story on to. It can be attached to products, create unrealistic aspirations, perpetuate myths and possibilities in glossy mags and on celluloid. Who wants to sell the reality of growing old?

The reality that the commercial world is so fearful of — the aches and pains and losses which accompany old age — is only part of the story. In these photographs I have tried not to avoid the battle-wounds and adversities of ageing, but I have emphasised the other side of the story – the wholeness and integrity of a continuing individual life with the youth still present in the eyes. It is this untold story that is life-enhancing, as I hope this book reveals.

The shape of this book is photograph-led. Women like Diana Athill and Joan Didion have written so perfectly about their late lives that I knew a book like this could only exist as a visual complement to those literary achieve-ments. Nonetheless, it does have a kind of narrative. The book starts with a general display of the variety of types of beauty. It moves on to look at the young person that still exists behind the image of an older women, and then to consider the attitudes young people have towards age. Next it shows images which prove that happiness and silliness are not the exclusive province of youth, but then shows some of the darker, tougher more sorrowful aspects of ageing. I then try to demonstrate how many storylines there are in women's faces and ask why we are not dramatising their stories or using the older actresses who could play them. Lastly I explore the question of how to grow old: first in the superficial sense of our appearance (to botox or not to botox), and then from the deeper aspect of how to look age in the eye and come to terms with it without going too gently.

I have been buoyed by the discovery of how absolutely welcome the exhibition has been for so many women. The generosity, the enthusiasm, the lack of vanity, the pleasure – the response has been amazing, both from the people who looked at the pictures and the women who allowed photographs of themselves to be displayed. I have been asked repeatedly if there would eventually be a publication of this kind, and hope therefore that this book affords an equivalent but different kind of pleasure to those who have responded so positively to the exhibition over the last few years, and to a new audience who encounter these images for the first time here.

Age cannot wither her, nor custom stale
Her infinite variety.

William Shakespeare,
Antony and Cleopatra (Act II scene ii)

Poh Sim Plowright | Georgia Oetker

20 Previous page left: **Sevil Peach Gence** | Neil Wilder
Previous page right: **Alison Beazley** | Sophie Lambe

Above: **Novella Nelson** | Georgia Oetker
Opposite: **Annie Lennox** | Lennox / Martin

Both images: **Caryl Churchill** | Stephen Cummiskey

Nila Bhupendra Vaghmaria | Sophie Lambe

Georgia Oetker | Simon Annand

Above: **Kate Littlewood** | Jill Kennington
Opposite: **Françoise Hardy** | François Durand/Rex Features

Sister Richardson | Joy Richardson

Noor Baba and **Susan Belgrave** | Jos Belgrave

Margaret Busby | Julian Rogers

Beautiful young people are accidents of nature,

Attributed to Eleanor Roosevelt

Phyllida Law | Georgia Oetker

but beautiful old people are works of art

You cannot call it love; for at your age
The hey-day in the blood is tame, it's humble
And waits upon the judgment:

William Shakespeare, Hamlet (Act III scene iv)

Above: **Adjoa Andoh** | Matt Writtle
Top: **Joan Bakewell** | Philip Reeson
Opposite: **Jane Birkin** | Karl Schoendorfer/Rex Features

Their hearts have not grown old;
Passion or conquest, wander where they will,
Attend upon them still.

W.B.Yeats, Wild Swans at Coole

Juanita Stickney | Drawing: Pietro Annigoni | Photograph: Jill Kennington

Inside every older person is a younger person wondering what the hell happened.

Cora Harvey Armstrong

Previous page left: **Pina Bausch** | Corbis
Previous page right: **Louise Galloway** | Katrin Talbot

One of the many things nobody ever tells you about middle age is that it's a nice change from being young.

Dorothy Canfield Fisher

Above: **Rohan McCullough** | Garlinda Birkbeck
Opposite: **Millie Laws** | Garlinda Birkbeck

Flagposts in the Ocean

According to my grandmother, when I was about 5 I asked a friend of hers how old she was. "Harriet, don't be rude!", hissed Granny. "It's quite alright", said her friend, "I'm as old as my heart and a little older than my teeth". A brilliant answer. The number of our age is for filling in forms and has little bearing on our inward experience.

In 1999 I was asked for a quote to mark the upcoming Millennium. I said something like: "Who's counting? Years are just flagposts in the ocean".

On New Year's Eve 1999, with a blazing bonfire in a friend's garden in North Yorkshire, I looked up into the arching dark and "ooohed and aaahed " as cascades of fireworks rushed giddyingly towards me and spattered the sky. Next morning I walked out into the new year and the new Millennium, following a crunchy path round a frozen pond and saw that the embers of the bonfire were still active and smouldering in the frosty beautiful morning. Day had followed night as it ever had and ever will and the sparrows had no clue that the Next Thousand Years had just begun.

I was born in 1950 and since early youth I had said – but not that often: "In the year 2000 I'll be 50". Now the year had arrived, and I spent my 50th birthday at a friend's house in Scotland, celebrating the christening of her child. The ceilidh went on into the night and whooped me over the hurdle into the day of my 50th. I smiled bravely as I cavorted. It was a celebration and I borrowed it.

Their hearts have not grown old;

W.B. Yeats, Wild Swans at Coole

Above: **Joyce Allery** and **Sybil Spinks** | David Ward
Opposite: **Judi Dench** and **Maggie Smith**, still from *Ladies in Lavender* (2004) | Georgia Oetker

Caroline Friend | Chris Bartle

Rosa Roballo | Harriet Walter

Eileen Hogan | Simon Annand

Above: **Caroline Montagu** | Harriet Walter

Top: **Lynn Goddard** | Patrick Baldwin

53

Old Girls

On a summer's day in 2000, the class of '67 from my boarding school gathered together for a reunion when we were all either just approaching or just past our 50th birthdays. When I first re-met these sister/strangers I saw a room full of middle-aged women – but within minutes, the veil of physical changes lifted from their faces and the seventeen year olds were revealed.

I think I've read somewhere that the part of the brain that recognises faces, hooks into certain almost eternal triangles: the triangle between the tip of the nose and the two cheekbones, the two eyebrows and the mouth, the two corners of the mouth and the chin. These proportions are distinctive in each individual and are largely unaffected by wrinkles, weight gain etc. I also recognised these 'girls' by their gestures, facial expressions, vocal idiosyncrasies – in short all the indicators of personality. In some people the essential teenage personality was very near the surface, whereas others were more resolutely 'grown up'. It took longer for the veil to lift off the latter.

It was often the case that the prettiest stars of the classroom had gone a bit dowdy while the naughty girls who spent their time messing about in the art room had become high-flyers, including a couple of accomplished musicians. Music was a big deal at my school, and it was therefore no surprise that, years on, we all gathered round and sang. I have photos of our greying heads clustered round with open-mouths, intensely singing madrigals. The school had introduced me to the pleasure of playing music and singing. It was one of the most valuable experiences I took away with me into my life. Now here we were doing exactly the same thing, less well but with greater enthusiasm.

We sat in a circle (it sounds awful but it wasn't) and one by one gave a brief resumé of our lives to date since leaving school. I was among the most nervous of speaking in public, something few but other actors would believe. We sat wrapt as people told of love and partnerships, experiments in careers, new generations produced, divorces, bereavements, nervous breakdowns, diseases, uprootings to foreign countries, books written, businesses started. I am sure that each of us was in some way thinking: "I don't believe this! I am 50! All this has happened to all of us!"

With a fluidity we could never re-create with any other group, we slid up and down the age spectrum, one minute middle-aged discussing the state of the education system, the next minute seventeen year olds recalling hilarious escapades and shrieking with laughter that sounded pretty much as it always had.

The seventeen year-olds stayed together all day and reluctantly parted and went back to our adult lives. When my photos of the day came back from the developers, I again saw a group of middle-aged women. The years had been frozen back in place.

Left to Right : **Penny Corke (Clarke), Helen Bucknall (Whitten), Veronica Tennant (Lister), Harriet Walter** | David Beales

If a face is allowed to age naturally, we see the child, the young and the old woman all at once, like the rings of a tree trunk. I tried to stretch this analogy to say that at the heart of the tree the green life continued to push outward while the exterior bark grew gnarled but a horticulturalist friend pointed out that it is actually the outer bark that is still living. At first I thought this new insight had destroyed my analogy, but on reflection I think it enhances it. What is seen as decay is actually evidence of ongoing life.

My Mother **Xandra** | Aged 3; Aged 40; Aged 70

Una Stubbs | Jill Kennington

You must not pity me because my sixtieth year finds me still astonished.
To be astonished is one of the surest ways of not growing old too quickly.

Sidonie Gabrielle Colette

I still feel young inside

I have intermittently written a diary throughout my life, far less often as I got older, and I have rarely reviewed what I wrote. However I did quite recently come across a Krapps Last Tape-style recording I had made when I was young, in which I ramble on into the microphone speaking to myself: "If you are listening to this, Harriet, when you are 50...". The way I said "50" indicated that I would have been surprised if my life would last that long, would last to that seemingly fictitious year 2000. Even at that early stage, I saw myself in a kind of dialogue with myself, forward and backward down the line of my life.

A dip into an old diary which I had written aged about 13 humbled/depressed/amazed me at how consistent the young person writing was with the person reading. In other words, age and experience had not actually sophisticated my thoughts as much as I would have expected them to have done. Philosophically, even intellectually, the woman I was to become, and still am, was pretty much formed. I vowed never to patronise 13 year olds again.

"I still feel young inside". I have heard that from so many people as they grow older. People in their 80s express the same disbelief at how old they have grown that a young person does on hitting their 30th birthday. Now that I know how that feels I vow never to patronise an 80 year old again.

Emma Thompson and **Phyllida Law** | Georgia Oetker

Stuckley: (a Knight) " ..Get on your cracking pins, you tottering old bugger"

Hush: (an old villager) "Thank you"

Stuckley: "Thank me why?"

Hush: "Because the worst thing in age is the respect. The smile of condescension, and the hush with which the most banal opinion is received."

Howard Barker, The Castle

We talked about growing old gracefully,
And Elsie who's seventy-four
Said, "A. It's a question of being sincere,
And B., If you're supple you've nothing to fear"
Then she swung upside-down from a glass chandelier!
I couldn't have liked it more!

Nöel Coward, I've Been to a Marvellous Party

Peggy Seeger | Dale Hubert

Can nobody be happy after they are quite young?

Gwendolen to her mother in Chapter 3 of Daniel Deronda by George Eliot

A Message to the Young

I decided one day to collect up some slogans from cosmetic bottles just to record some of their impossible claims for rejuvenation. To this end I was squatting in an aisle in Boots jotting down various claims, my favourites being: 'reverse the ageing process'; 'be younger 7 times faster'; and 'abolish those elevens' ('the elevens' being the 2 parallel vertical furrows between the eyebrows), when I overheard a conversation between a mother and a daughter who were also cruising the shelves for face creams. "Here, this one says 'deep night time moisturiser'". "Oh Mum, no!" moaned the younger voice, "It doesn't say anything about wrinkles. I want an anti-wrinkle cream." I looked up to see the speaker was a peachy-skinned woman in her 20s talking to an attractive 50-something mother whose example, I would have thought, gave her little cause for dread.

When young people pity the old and fear getting older, it's hard to hang on to one's own conviction that growing older has its compensations. But sometimes I want to tell the young that youth isn't all it's cracked up to be. Depression and disillusionment are rife amongst young people, and it can be one of the hardest times of your life, especially when people tell you it should be the best. The young can be under the greatest of pressures with the least access to control over their own lives.

I want to tell them they will have more confidence as they grow older, that they will be able to laugh at – even pity – the setters of those standards they feel they fall short of.

I want to tell them they won't always have to try to look perfect, that they can aspire to a different kind of beauty: the beauty of survival and tenacity and humour and patience and lived-in-ness. I want them to look forward to a time when they don't get periods any more and can have sex without ever worrying about getting pregnant, and that they can one day admit it if they don't even like sex that much.

I want to tell them that in so many ways life gets better and that my 40s and 50s have been some of the best times in my life and I look forward to more. A friend who re-met and married the love of her life in her 80s told me that this was the happiest time of her life. It was inspiring to realise that someone in the latter phase of her life could still perceive the present as expanding and fruitful.

Sandra de Laszlo and **grand children** | Garlinda Birkbeck

The trouble is that however hard older women try to put things in perspective for the young it won't really have any reality for them. The old can remember being young, middle-aged and old, and can dispense advice from all those vantage points. For the young, who have only ever been young, there are no short cuts. They will have to find things out the hard way, just as we did. The best we can expect is that they will remember the odd useful tip about later life so that it rings true by the time they need it.

There is an old French proverb: 'Si jeunesse savait, si vieillesse pouvait', which roughly translates as 'If Youth only knew and if Age only could', which seems to sum up this never-closing arc. I recently found a comment on this proverb on a French website: 'Mais si jeunesse savait, elle n'oserait pas, et si vieillesse pouvait, il n'y aurait pas de place pour les jeunes. A chacun son moment.' Meaning: 'If Youth had the knowledge it wouldn't dare use it; and if Age had the power, there would be no place for the young. To each their time.'

Indu Khambhaita | Sophie Lambe

Above: **Louise Galloway** | Katrin Talbot
Opposite: **Maggie Scott** | Laurent Moulin

Old Dog New Tricks

I took up riding again recently. It was always something that both terrified and thrilled me. I remember the day my mother rather sadly announced that her riding days were over. She had slipped a disc and though she had recovered she decided it was too risky to ride again. She was still in her 40s.

I had never been a habitual rider so I presumed that like my mother I had ridden my last horse many years ago. But then there I was a couple of years back careering across a beach in Ireland at a speed that, in my experience, only paralleled riding pillion on a motorbike. I could barely gulp the air, could hardly see what direction I was going in with my eyes screwed up against the beating wind. When I drew my horse up and we both stood panting, I was struck by the exhilarating thought that it had all come back to me and I hadn't fallen off!

I had been almost tricked into this ride (and out of my fear) by some friends who had been brought up with horses and treated the whole thing as easy and natural. I decided to carry on doing it when I got home to England.

I borrowed some gear and booked into a local riding stables, but I soon discovered that in this more formal English situation, the horses were trained to respond to quite specific and different signals from the ones I was taught in my youth. The Irish horses hadn't seemed to mind but, anyway, I decided to have a 'Group Lesson'.

The 'group' consisted of two nine-year old girls with straight slender legs, dressed in creaseless clothes and pastel silk riding hats. As they trotted their neat little ponies round the ring, I felt like a giant pillock.

I had to learn some totally new tricks about posture and commands. My body was put through every contortion and I couldn't for the life of me see the logic. "Grip with your knees! Toes up, heels down!", they had always shouted in my youth, and that was what my body automatically did. Now it was: "Get those legs back! The horse must feel your lower leg in touch with his flank at all times or he won't take you seriously! Don't lean forward! Don't stick your bottom out!". Well *you* try keeping your legs back so your heels are level with your hips without tilting forward with your bum sticking out!

At the end of the session the teacher had the grace to absolve me in front of the nine-year olds: "It's much harder for Harriet having to un-learn what she has always known and start from scratch than it is for you girls who are learning for the first time."

On my way home, anticipating the next few days' agony and feeling gloomy about my failure, I wondered why I should have to learn new tricks when I had always ridden perfectly well. Why couldn't this new horse learn some old tricks?

Previous page L to R: **Betty Blythe, Sheila Holdsworth, Alice O'Donnell** | Jill Kennington
This page: **Keep Fit Class** | Jill Kennington

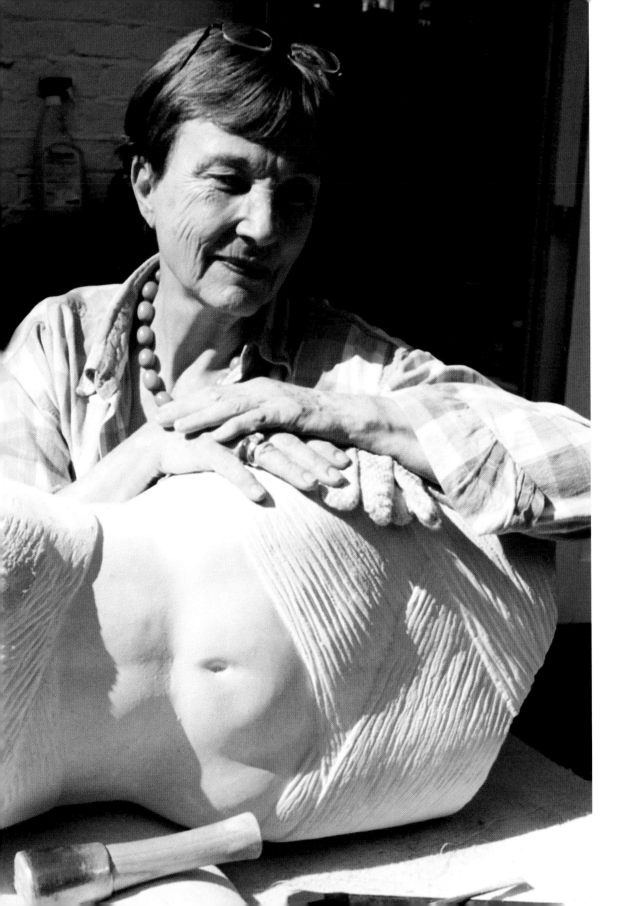

Above: **Rose Goodwin** | Carolyn Hailstones

Opposite: **Christine Sapieha Fremantle** | Jill Kennington

Susan

Susan is the mother of a woman I was at school with. Mother and daughter came backstage to visit me during the run of a play I was doing at a time when my partner was terminally ill. I hadn't been able to tell anyone about this within the acting profession and so I found myself blurting it out to these women whom I hardly knew. Susan was strong, unembarrassed and positive. She told me that when her husband died she decided to do those things she hadn't been able to do with him – either because they were too busy or because he wouldn't have enjoyed them. So for the last ten years or so she had been off on riding adventures in remote parts of the world; the Hindu Kush, Mongolia, Kyrgyzstan and the like.

"Now that's the sort of thing I should do", I enthused: "Well, why don't you?". I interpreted this as a challenge. I felt Susan would judge me as ily-livered if I didn't give it a try. Intermittently, when we met over the next couple of years, Susan would nudge me with a reminder: "When are you coming on a ride?"

Then in early 2008, she announced: "The next trip leaves for Kyrgyzstan in June". I realised that very few of my excuses ("What if a job comes up?"; "Not sure I have the money"; "Not sure I'm a good enough rider"), would wash with Susan, but June seemed miles away.

When May arrived, which was the last moment for acquiring a visa, I decided to get one just in case. It was only when I walked away from the Kyrgyzstan Consulate and started buying insecticide at Boots that I realised I had decided to go.

In my own head, my main excuse had been: "Going on riding adventures just isn't me." But, having done it, I realise how wrong one can be about who 'me' is, and at high altitudes, staring out over roadless villageless miles and miles, 'me' doesn't really come into it.

Opposite both images: **Susan Belgrave** | Jos Belgrave

Our first day driving up to the horses. We got out of the car to stretch our legs. Susan rejoiced at returning to Kyrgyzstan. When we got back to the car she said: "I can hold it in my heart now. One day I won't be able to come back."

Above left: **Susan Belgrave** | Harriet Walter

Above right: **Susan Belgrave** | Jos Belgrave

Opposite top: **Susan practising the Russian that she had started learning in her late 70s early 80s** | Jos Belgrave

Opposite bottom: **Easing aching limbs in Lake Issy Kul after 12 days on horseback.** | Hugo Berkeley

Cicely Berry | Ellie Kurttz

One thing I love about being 80 is having fewer fears and I daily thank god I am blessed with health, loving relationships and enough money. Another thing I love is the solicitude of the young. Often, they address me in a special voice and ask how I'm keeping as if in anticipation of my imminent decay. "Take care" is the usual valediction, and I duly resolve not to trip, hurry, or do anything illegal out of dottiness. I love the world, its people and places and the arts that inform and illuminate it. I love parties, travel, clothes, and cock a snook at the Grim Reaper with my expensive haircut. My old mind is a bulging stockroom and whatever happens currently there are connections to be made with all that stuff in my head.

Margaret Freeman-Attwood, The Times, 20 October 2003

Old age is no place for cissies

Attributed to Bette Davis

Pity us human beings, the only species (we think) that is aware of its own mortality, knowing that death gets closer and closer with every tick of the second hand. How brave to look that fact in the eye and in spite of it, still get up in the morning, go on building and loving and putting down roots.

Opposite both images: **Rhona Kennington** | Jill Kennington

Sarina de Mayo | Rupert Burrows

Tessa Verrechia and **Merelina Kendall** | Sophie Lambe

Letting go

Ageing is a great leveller. I have found that, on the whole, people get kinder to one another as they grow older. We are not so inclined to say: "It's alright for *her*", because by now we know that it's never *all* right for any of us. Bereavements, transitions, adjustments are not for cissies, and so many of the most drastic changes happen nearest to the end of life when we are physically at our weakest. One could argue that precisely because of that weakness it is a good time to shed some of the load. Preparing for getting old involves letting go of things and habits of mind and, the hardest of all, people.

Elsbeth Juda | Georgia Oetker

How many loved your moments of glad grace,
And loved your beauty with love false or true,
But one man loved the pilgrim soul in you,
And loved the sorrows of your changing face;

William Butler Yeats, When You are Old

Opposite: **Cleo Laine** | Jill Kennington

Odette Coker | Sophie Lambe

There is nothing more satisfying, more gratifying than true adulthood. The process of becoming one is not inevitable. Its achievement is a difficult beauty, an intensely hard-won glory, which commercial forces and cultural vapidity should not be permitted to deprive you of.

Toni Morrison

Sheila Hancock | Harriet Walter

Merelina Kendall and **grandson Seamus** | Sophie Lambe

Someone to wave Goodbye

"They come back" People told me. "They'll rip your heart out leaving, but they come back." Mine won't, I thought. I wasn't the first to think that, though I didn't know it then.

Yet here you are, going, though you live here yet. You no longer see me, your gaze on the horizon. You are all ready at the frontier, leaving only a shirttail in my grasp.

Your adventures are your own. You no longer share them, as I no longer plan them. It's my life, you say, and I know that. But yet but yet but yet...

I can't see what you do, your vision unclouded by compromise. I try to tell you I saw that way once. I might as well say eat your vegetables. The way you pay attention.

But I didn't always tend this safe nest – I too lived on the outlaw border. But that was a different adventure.

Not yours.

Strange, how cruelty is not in you, but still you leave with bits of bloody heart in your talons.

They come back.

Yes, but it will be from places I'll never know, a frontier I can not visit, and when you show me the snapshots, I'll not see them, too busy tracing a baby's brow in a young laugh.

I too, once lived on the outlaw border. Saw clear-eyed. Yet, I never needed courage more than now. Saying Go.

Trusting someone will come back.

S.E. Hinton

One Art

The art of losing isn't hard to master;
so many things seem filled with the intent
to be lost that their loss is no disaster.

Lose something every day. Accept the fluster
of lost door keys, the hour badly spent.
The art of losing isn't hard to master.

Then practice losing farther, losing faster:
places, and names, and where it was you meant
to travel. None of these will bring disaster.

I lost my mother's watch. And look! my last, or
next-to-last, of three loved houses went.
The art of losing isn't hard to master.

I lost two cities, lovely ones. And, vaster,
some realms I owned, two rivers, a continent.
I miss them, but it wasn't a disaster.

– Even losing you (the joking voice, a gesture
I love) I shan't have lied. It's evident
the art of losing's not too hard to master
though it may look like (*Write* it!) a disaster.

Elizabeth Bishop

Melanie McFadyean | Jenny Matthews

If it takes a near-death experience for you to appreciate your life, you're wasting somebody's time

Nikki Giovanni, poet and Civil Rights activist

The Skoda

In 2004 I lost my partner, the actor Peter Blythe. As I pieced my life back together over the next years I wrote the following:

It is about time I sold my Skoda. It still runs perfectly but on the outside it is pretty disfigured. I decided not to spend money on its outside appearance since it gets me where I need to get to and is a friendly nest inside. I have left the scratches some joker's key inflicted on its flank, and the dent under the front where I hit a badger. Someone will give me a couple of hundred pounds for it, touch up the bodywork and sell it on; there is life in it still.

It has been my home through four years of batting up and down to London and across the country, no distance too far to go to see a friend, or go to an event. I have spent as much time in that car over the last four years as any other single place apart from my bed. I have had long conversations in it, with myself, with friends, and most importantly with my late partner Peter. Conversations, silences, hilarious laughter and one memorable screaming row are all bottled in that cabin. All that energy pursed up in that little tin room on wheels - you realise how tiny it is when you are in the car wash and you can't see out.

I have had famous people in the passenger seat and I have done over 50,000 miles in it. But above all, I am sentimentally attached to the car because Peter sat in the passenger seat in sickness and in health and after he died I howled with pain in that comforting shell where no one could see or hear me.

In the end I gave it to my goddaughter, who, unburdened by any knowledge of its history, was delighted to have my old banger as her 'first new car'.

Harriet Walter and **The Skoda** | A passer by

A lifetime of kissing, of speaking and weeping, shows expressively around a mouth scored like a leaf in motion.

Naomi Wolf, The Beauty Myth

Opposite: **Erminia Bazzano** | Jeremy Finlay

Look Again

Our faces drop and droop as we get older. It is a law of gravity. Sorrow and worry etch themselves on our brows as well as laughter round our mouths and eyes. They say that after 50 we get the face we deserve but the truth is less convenient than that. Our genes have an equal, if not greater input. A sweet looking little old lady could be a selfish pain in the …, a sour-faced granny could break into an adorable smile. I often wrongly judge the mask.

There's no art to find the mind's construction in the face.
William Shakespeare, Macbeth (Act 1 scene iv)

Across the way on the tube I see a grumpy-looking woman in her 60s. Set in her ways and narrow-minded, I instantly decide. Then she gets a book out of her bag. "Dirty Russian: Everyday slang from 'What's up?' to 'F*%# Off'"

In a New York café I see an old woman with her carer sitting at a table. Not a word passes between them as the old lady fiddles with her food. I write the scenario: The old lady is a spoilt racist and her black carer bitterly resents having to care for her in order to earn enough to look after her own children. When I look back in their direction some time later, the carer is gently wiping the old lady's mouth and murmuring sweet nothings in her ear. On their way out, something sets the pair of them off giggling. Through the window, I watch them hobble off down the street in a dumbshow of continuing hilarity. I promise always to look again.

Within the pages of this book there are the faces of women whose experiences are invisible to us. Amongst them there are those that have nursed a dying son or daughter, those who have always lived with a severe disability, there are sufferers and survivors of cancer, a few that have lived with the threat of torture and imprisonment. One woman lost her entire family in the Blitz when she was 18. At least two are in the early stages of Alzheimer's or are nursing a partner with the disease.

But there is also more than one woman who carried on painting into her 90s, a 70 year old who has taken up the cello, a survivor of breast cancer who taught herself to fly. There are women who have discovered new love in a relationship with another woman. There are women who are letting their hair down for the first time in decades, seeing the positive side of the empty nest. They are letting themselves off the 'perfect wife and mother' hook, and confessing to past misdemeanours: dope-smoking, shop-lifting, adultery… Which one is which is irrelevant. We just look again, salute them and know that we cannot know the half of it.

Christine Sapieha Fremantle and cat | Jill Kennington

Your face, my thane, is as a book where men
May read strange matters.

William Shakespeare, Macbeth (Act I scene v)

I haven't asked you to make me young again. All I want is to go on getting older.

Konrad Adenauer to his doctor

Above: **Angharad Miskin** | Jill Kennington
Opposite: **Mrs Pollington** and **Miss Pollington** | Jill Kennington

The days and the months pace over us like restless little birds, and leave the marks of their feet backwards and forwards; especially when they are like birds with heavy hearts – then they tread heavily.

George Eliot, Daniel Deronda

It's not about us

It has become a common complaint among actresses (and increasingly among women in the audience) and I am proudly adding to the clamour: "There are not enough parts for women! Let alone older women!" Why is it that drama has seldom reflected the fact that women make up half the population, and an ageing population at that? Why is it hard to place older women in the story and why is the story practically never *about* them? Why can't the fascinating lives of some of the women in these portraits be dramatised? There are so many brilliant and under-used actresses who could play them. Why are older women passed by on the street? Why don't we look again and ask them about themselves?

The classical repertoire can be excused on grounds of the social mores of the time, but now? Without the excuses of the past, why do we still seem to have a problem getting stories about older women past the pitching point? It is a vicious circle. There are fewer roles for women, fewer actresses

Carmen Maura, still from *Volver* (2006) | Rex Features

therefore make enough films to become international names, and few films can be made without international names attached.

The English-speaking cinema woos a young audience and makes the assumption that no one is interested in an older woman's story. But a good story is a good story, and occasionally a story surfaces that blows everyone's assumptions away. Usually these sneak up on us from the independent or foreign film market, from a culture where women can still be considered sexy in their 50s and 60s and interesting for other things than sex appeal way beyond those years.

Mainstream cinema is built on aspiration, sexual fantasy, identification, hopes and dreams and "In a dream you are never 80", as the poet Anne Sexton points out. Is this the problem? That a story about a middle-aged or old person has too little future? When we walk into the distance as the credits roll, is the road ahead too short for that feel-good factor? Do the male Hollywood powers reject stories based on older women because they place themselves imaginatively in the hero's shoes and want to get the girl, not the older woman closer to their own age? Do female Hollywood powers not want to look too closely at their own destiny?

Whatever the reasons, the people who enable films to get made have done endless research on audiences, and they tell us that youth is the largest demographic group watching and buying films, *ergo* they invest in films that the young want to see. So those who want different kinds of films can just wait for the odd exception to slip through the net: Julie Christie in *Away From Her,* Vanessa Redgrave in *Evening*, Judi Dench in *Iris*. Pity they all happen to be dying or have Alzheimer's. Some recent movies, *Mamma Mia, The Kids are Alright, Something's Gotta Give,* all centre on fabulous 50 year old and sexy 60 year old women, and have done brilliantly at the box office, so let's have more! "Write a screenplay yourself", they say to us. But that is to underestimate the huge and specialised skill that takes. I tried it once and wrote myself the most boring part imaginable! Who will dramatise these women's stories?

122 **Anna Ford** | Bill Knight

Above: **Joëlle Mnouchkine** | Sanya Ballerini

Top: **Lucinda Childs** | Georgia Oetker

Chloe Fremantle | Jil Kennington

Hillary Rohde | Garlinda Birkbeck

Happiness depends on being free, and freedom depends on being courageous.

Thucydides, History of the Peloponnesian War

Maysoon Pachachi | Eugenie Dolberg

Veronica Stewart and friends | David Ward

There's a new phenomenon: the emotional vitality of woman at a certain age. When you go into your sixties, you're looking forward as well as back at a great experience of life.

David Hare, programme notes on his play, The Breath of Life

Bianca Jagger | Toby Melville /Reuters

I was so much older then; I'm younger than that now.

Bob Dylan

Patti Love | Harriet Walter

Peggy Seeger in concert | Ursy Potter

Louise Gibbings | Garlinda Birkbeck

A Joke:

A couple are celebrating their 50th wedding anniversary. The Fairy Godmother turns up and asks each of them to make one wish which she will grant them.

She turns to the wife. "What is your wish?"
"Well" says the wife, "I know I'm getting old, so I would like a completely new kitchen, fitted so that I can use it easily if I end up in a wheelchair; reachable taps, cupboards, shelves. Smoothed off corners so I won't hurt myself, easy to clean surfaces etc."

"Fine" says the Fairy Godmother and waves her wand. "Abracadabra!" and there instantly appeared before her a perfect user-friendly kitchen. The wife was delighted.

"Now you" said the Fairy Godmother, turning to the husband, "What is your wish?" "Well," said the husband, moving closer to the Fairy Godmother so he could speak in a sotto voce, confidential tone "I'd like a wife 20 years younger than me." "Simple" said the Fairy Godmother, and she waved her wand.

"Abracadabra!"…and the man was 90 years old.

They told me 'Advertising is for dreams, not reality, and women dream to be young.' That was their reasoning. It's wrong, of course. Not all women want to be blonde, thin and young. But that's the image companies want to sell. And you always have to fight it.

Isabella Rossellini, on being sacked by Lancôme

Opposite: **Mary Quant** | Jill Kennington

Above left: **Nomanono Isaacs** | Jill Kennington
Above right: **Claudia Stolze** | Harriet Walter
x

Above left: **Nomanono Isaacs** | Jill Kennington
Above right: **Claudia Stolze** | Harriet Walter
Opposite: **Moira Stuart** | David Fisher/Rex Features

Con de Hamel | Jill Kennington

Father Time is not always a hard parent, and, though he tarries for none of his children, often he lays his hand lightly upon those who have used him well: making them old men and women inexorably enough, but leaving their hearts and spirits young and in full vigour.
With such people the grey head is but the impression of the old fellow's hand in giving them his blessing, and every wrinkle but a notch in the quiet calendar of a well-spent life.

Charles Dickens, Barnaby Rudge

You've got a simple choice, girls: get old or look creepy

Tina Fey

Anita Pallenberg, who I remembered from the film *Performance* as having the 'IT' look of the age, has retained so much of that rock chic youthful quality while embracing what she called her 'battlescars', the lines and deep scores of age.

Opposite: **Anita Pallenberg** | Jill Kennington

It's like two tribes:
The botox tribe thinks: "Why doesn't she do something?" And the other side thinks: "They look scalded. They look bizarre."
Meryl Streep

I don't think ageing is easy for anyone; it takes a lot of courage to grow old and not have plastic surgery. I haven't had any work done, but I have mixed feelings about it. There are times when I would like to be helped because, on the big screen, things are accentuated as you get older. But I also feel that my face is my conscience; and I do think that, somewhere in your heart, you've got to be at peace with yourself.

Jacqueline Bisset

'Noooo. I love the gift I've been given. I don't want to get to Heaven and St Peter to say: 'Who the Hell are you?' I want him to see wrinkles, grey hair, double belly, double chin, arms that jiggle, thighs that rub together, big feet…it's me.'
Mo'nique, (Stand up comic and talk show hostess, as well as winner of best supporting Oscar for Precious, when asked if she would contemplate plastic surgery.)

We all feel young inside - getting older is fine if you are healthy. I've had operations for lung and throat cancer. I am not prepared to have unnecessary operations for face-lift
Sylvie Cristel

I remember ten years ago a woman in America –
and she was referring to me and to herself –
saying: 'Well, this is what 40 looks like!' Meaning,
'Don't we look marvellous!' And I said, 'Well it's
only what 40 looks like if you've had an easy life,
with enough to eat and someone to do your hair
and make-up'. It's such a narrow view. The nar-
cissism of it still upsets me… And it's no good just
saying, 'Oh but I don't want to be part of that' and
then giving in. As Gandhi said, you've got to be
part of the change you want to see happen.

Emma Thompson

148   **Jill Kennington** | Sylvain Guenot

We have to ask ourselves whether we really want to paralyse our facial muscles, wipe away all signs of age and accept that only by looking oddly youthful for as long as possible are we allowed any place in public life. If we do, then we're bending to a viciously sexist and ageist ideal. And, let's face it, obedience is never a good look

Kira Cochrane

Mrs Candour: she's 53 or 53 at the utmost- and I don't think she looks more

Sir Benjamin: ah! There's no judging by her looks, unless one could see her face

Lady Sneerwell: Well, if Mrs Evergreen does take some pains to repair the ravages of time, you must allow she effects it with great ingenuity; and surely that's better than the careless manner in which the widow Ochre caulks her wrinkles.

Sir Benjamin: Nay, now, Lady Sneerwell, you are severe upon the widow. Come, come, 'tis not that she paints so ill- but when she has finished her face, she joins it on so badly to her neck, that she looks like a mended statue, in which the connoisseur may see at once that the head is modern though the trunk's antique.

Mrs Candour: Ha! Ha! Ha! Well, you make me laugh; but I vow I hate you for it.

Richard Brinsley Sheridan, The School for Scandal (Act II scene ii)

We need our faces

Maybe it is because so many of my friends are actors who need their faces to tell the truth that I have found them so sympathetic to this book. To them plastic surgery (or too much of it) would be a re-writing of their history. They would rather get to know and even like their changing ageing faces and bodies than lose their history and their selves.

I salute their bravery because the pressure on actresses to look young is enormous. For those who can afford access to the very top surgeons it may just be possible to have work done that is so subtle that we can't detect it. However High Definition Technology is now the norm in films and tv, and even the most beautiful young stars can look better off screen than on. HD is fine for photographing the mating habits of mosquitoes on wildlife pro- grammes but no human, however ravishing, can survive that kind of scrutiny.

Vanessa Redgrave | Sandra Lousada

In the US and increasingly here in Britain, so many women have had work done that they have lost their bearings. They have literally lost sight of what they used to look like, their 'real' face, and walk around with what looks to me like a mask of fear – ironically more of a memento mori than the lines they try so hard to iron out. It has almost got to the point that when I see a very peeled and plumped up 'worked-on' face I assume the person is in their 70s when they may be only 55.

Stop Looking at Yourself in the Mirror!

There was a mirror in the hallway and we were about to go out, not to a party or anything where I had to look good, just shopping or something. "Stop looking at yourself in the mirror", Peter exclaimed. He was right. I did (do) look in the mirror a lot, but I had to explain to him that it wasn't simple vanity, it was a reality check. I am on the cusp of old age and I can see the child, the young woman and the old woman in me. We are the only animals who are conscious of what we look like and our metamorphoses can be quite traumatic. The change to old from youngish can be sudden, a *coup de vieux* as the French say, comparable to the change for an adolescent boy from sweet child to pimply youth.

I seemed to bumble along with much the same self-image (I didn't look in the mirror so much) from 35-50, but now the alterations come quite rapidly. I am trying to square the continuum of my felt inner self with the physically changing outer case I see in the mirror — the only version of me that others can experience.

In a way it is part of my job. Casting directors see me as I appear now. The Ophelias and Juliets, the Hedda Gablers that I used to play are irrelevant. What is the commodity that I am now? I look in the mirror and try to see myself how others see me, what story it is telling.

A woman surprised by time

Sir Walter Raleigh speaking of Queen Elizabeth I

I feel like picture A, which doesn't seem so far from picture B, but I often get seen as picture C.

Pic **A**: Me now by Georgia Oetker.

Picture **B**: Me aged 25

Picture **C**: still from *Trial and retribution* (2005)

I find this shocking. I try to work against it. I laugh and smile as much as possible but in repose I look sad or stern. Where has all that laughter and affability been stored in my face? I am up against my inherited facial mould.

Another problem is that my face and I keep different hours. I am quite good in the morning when I *look* like shit and my face gets better and better throughout the day, peaking late at night when I *feel* like shit.

I try to get used to my image in the mirror so as to cushion the shock I will inevitably experience when I next see myself on film. (P.S. Due to deteriorating eyesight, the shock is even greater with my specs on.)

Cynthia 'Cy' O'Neil | Harriet Walter

I come from a generation that never thought we would grow up, let alone get wise. So in order to avoid it we all dress like kids, we hit the gym and thanks to certain moisturisers and professional men's savvy with a surgical hacksaw we can look young almost till death. No matter what has to be stapled, sewn up or sucked out, the silent message that ain't so silent is: 'Be young, free and don't tell anyone how old you are.' Wisdom is never mentioned in *Vogue* and no one is requesting it at Harvey Nichols.

Ruby Wax, How do you want me?

Daphne Selfe | Alexandra Myers

Having it all

We, the baby-boomers, are getting our bus passes. We like these advantages but we also want to hang on to the advantages of our youth. Most of us are a lot better off than most of the young. We fight for the right to keep active and sell our skills in the market-place. We are in tension against the young who are finding it hard to get on to the property ladder, the career ladder – or to leave home and get any job at all. I am torn between contesting the ageism that kicks older women out of jobs they are still good at, and letting the young have their turn.

The have-it-all generation that feels it invented youth in the 1960s is reluctant to let it go. We hitch up our faces and tuck them behind our ears. We get praise for preserving the silhouette of our 30 year old selves and for fitting into the jeans we wore 15 years ago. We want to be the eternal Rock 'n' Roll generation.

On the other hand some of us are quite OK about getting old. It is quite a relief not to have to try for perfection in our appearance. What is beautiful about youth is youth itself – the glow, the gloss, the smooth contours, the promise, the potential. We've all had that, even though we didn't appreciate it then. No amount of skilful surgery can give make us as beautifully young as the young, so why try?

Once you reach a certain age you're not allowed to be adventurous, you're not allowed to be sexual. I mean, is there a rule? Are you supposed to just die?

Madonna

Decisions, decisions...

How to grow old and when? In the past it was so much easier. Girls wore their hair long and loose till they got married when they tied it up. Matrons wore matronly clothes and widows wore black. Old women wore bonnets and shawls. Now the choice is all ours:

To botox or not to botox? The face or the figure? To slow down and go easier on ourselves, or run to catch up with lost time? To care more about our appearance because it needs more work, or to get easier about it and find vanity self-indulgent and irrelevant?

I *think* I have decided that health matters above all at this stage in my life and that personal hygiene is a must for other people's sake (which kind of depends on having a *mentis* that is *compos* enough to care and eyes good enough to see the crumbs on one's chin, or the goo in one's eye). Other than that it is all up to me.

The role models I have selected in this book inspire me to try looking good for my age, rather than young. Waxing legs, plucking eyebrows and chin whiskers, dyeing hair, a good haircut, good food and not too much of it, enough sleep, clothes that make you feel good but not uncomfortable, shoes you can run for a bus in, that don't give you backache or blisters (take the teetery heels in a plastic bag to put on at the party); these are all on my own OK list.

My grandmother spent most of her day in bed when she got very old but coiled her hair into a chignon, powdered her nose and wore lipstick, high heels, gloves and a veil to go to the local shops once a day.

That was her choice. I wonder what I will do if I live that long. I suspect I will see-saw as I do now between looking like a slob when what I am doing is more important than how I am looking, and brushing up nice for special occasions.

Jane Birkin and **Charlotte Rampling** | François Durand/Rex Features

How foolish to think one could ever slam the door in the face of age. Much wiser to be polite and gracious and ask him to lunch in advance.

Nöel Coward

Above: **Leila Seth** | Aradhana Seth

Opposite: **Louise Galloway** and **Tianne McCoy** | Katrin Talbot

Come on, Norma, wake up! You're a woman of 50. There's nothing tragic about being 50, not unless you're trying to be 25

From Sunset Boulevard (1950), directed by Billy Wilder

Paola Fletcher | Garlinda Birkbeck

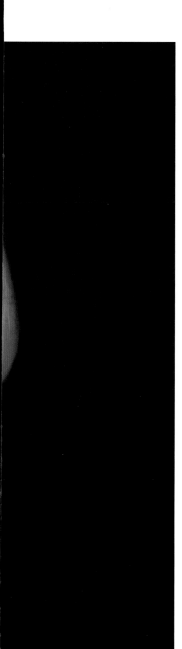

Fagabonds

I happened to be driving through Taunton recently and something caught my eye as I pulled up at the traffic lights.

A group of what looked to be a coach-load of elderly day-trippers, with pastel cardies and tight perms, were gathered outside the Mecca Bingo building, some standing, some sitting on the steps, all sharing an illicit fag, a laugh and a natter with a bunch of tattooed construction workers in sweaty T-shirts and hard hats. Strange bedfellows brought together by the smoking ban.

Fighting against the Tide

I remember a debate on television in which Michele Hanson, staunch champion of getting old naturally, sat across the table from a male plastic surgeon, and challenged his position. Michele suggested to the plastic surgeon that his industry made money out of women's (and now men's) insecurity.

His defence was that cosmetic surgery was all getting safer and more affordable, and that if he could make a woman feel better about herself he considered he had done a good thing.

We should challenge a culture that makes women feel better about themselves if they have been surgically altered, a culture that stigmatises and is repelled by old age and whose values we so often internalise against ourseleves.

Women, more than men, have had a lifelong training in deriving happiness or misery from their idea of how they are seen. It is a hard habit to break but a necessary one. What we look like should not be what makes us happy or unhappy, and looking like an unrecognisable plastic clone is no route to contentment.

We should fight against the tide; not the tide of time and age, which is a battle we can't win, but the media tide that tells us only youth is valuable, sexy or interesting, because only youth is beautiful and only beauty is sexy and only sexy is interesting. They do a great job of convincing us that only the young can be happy and if we counter them, they tell us we must be in denial.

The cosmetics and fashion industries prey on our vanities and fears. OK, but give them a break. That is their job. We do have a choice to take that stuff or leave it. It is a market after all. I can confidently pick what I want off the supermarket shelf or choose what I feel like eating from a menu. The waiter doesn't challenge what I want and tell me to eat something else that I don't want. That is because I order with assurance. But when it comes to fashion or beauty products, we seem to lose our confidence and common sense and become susceptible to a load of baloney.

Opposite: **Jean Muir** | Jill Kennington

Margo: Oh Leila.. Wasn't she horrible! Tell me - is there any truth in what she said? Am I slipping? Am I on the way out?

Leila: Don't be silly, Baby. You're the greatest. Pure gold. That one's just brass.

Margo: There was some truth in what she said. I do need pink lights.

Leila: She'll need 'em too some day, unless someone kills her before she gets that old... About them pink lights - there's only one way to meet old age.

Look it in the eye.

From All About Eve (1950)
based on a short story, The Wisdom of Eve by Mary Orr

Amelia Scimone | Micaela Scimone

The 'O' word

We should be pleased to have survived into old age. Shall we reclaim the word 'old' just as black people are proud to be black, and as gay people have reinvented the term 'gay'. Can we rid the term of its pejorative meanings and imbue it with a new vigour and dignity?

I overheard a conversation at a memorial the other day:
Person A: "He must be as old as you are, isn't he?"
Person B: "Well THANK you! If I weren't in a church I'd swipe you!"

Then there are those times when someone says: "Somebody of your age… Oops, sorry!", all said very jovially – but what is the supposed insult?

I have been alive for 60 years and I cannot find it in myself to be insulted when people remind of that fact. I am an older woman, and there you are. And yet I notice that I have used the word 'older'. I slip the 'er' on the end as a buffer, a gentle braking, a cushioning of the negative connotations which the word 'old' too starkly carries. I will embrace it yet.

Mary, one of the oldest sitters for the photographic exhibition, is practically blind, so I accompanied the photographer I had commissioned to take her portrait on her first visit to Mary's home in a little country village. They got on swimmingly and at the end of the session Mary asked the photographer how old she was. The photographer answered that she was 48. The old lady expressed surprise: "I thought you were about thirty!". "Thank you! I'm flattered!" said the photographer, the usual polite response. Mary's immediate reply was a simple and surprising, "Why?"

It is a proven fact that I am old, but if I refer to myself as an old woman, people around me start chorusing, "Youre not old" – consoling me, reassuring me, denying the obvious. They think I am disparaging myself, doing myself down. But I am not a gerontophobe: 66, by any computation, is old. I call myself old by way of combating the prevailing gerontophobia.

Germaine Greer

No spring, nor summer hath such grace
As I have seen in one autumnal face.
Were her first years the Golden Age, that's true,
But now she's gold oft tried, and ever new.

John Donne, The Autumnall

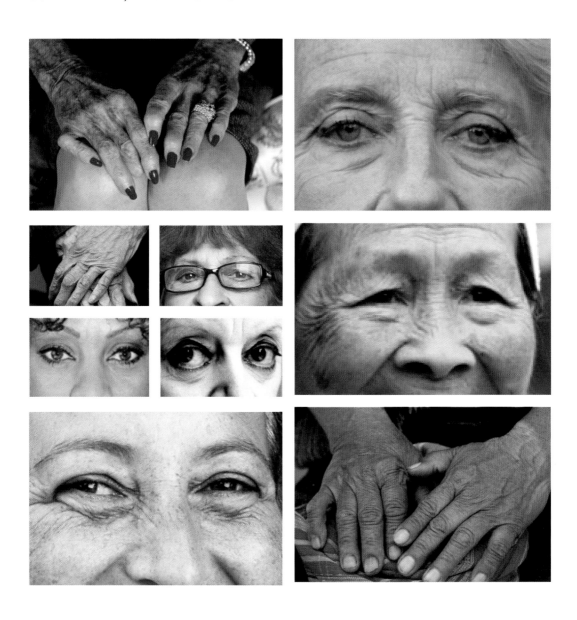

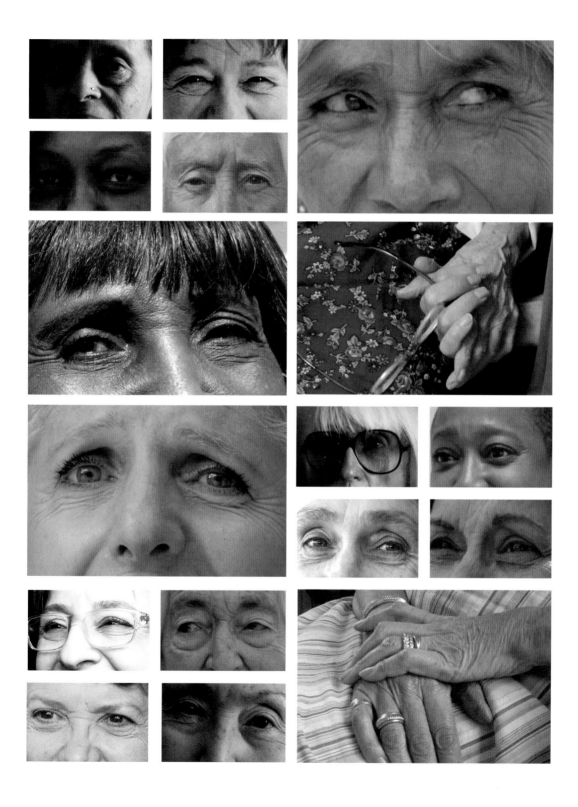

The Unmentionable

Old age is full of stigmas. In their stoicism, the old generally protect us from their experience of various unmentionables: loneliness, illness, depression and poverty. Loneliness is probably the hardest one to mention and the most pervasive. I have had a good taste of it, as I am sure most people have, and one feels a kind of patheticness one is too proud to admit. Loneliness does not discriminate between age groups but to be lonely at the end of one's life must be worst of all. We should be able to tell old people that they can drop the brave face sometimes, that they are not alone or on a different planet. We are all alone together.

I worry that many older people don't get touched enough. When Peter died I started to rehearse never being touched lovingly again. I wrote the following during that time.

It feels like love

A special offer comes through my letter box. It is from my local Beauty Salon. I have been there a few times and they know from some record or other that I have just had a birthday and so they have sent me a Special Birthday offer which is only valid for 10 days after my birthday. I have just realized that today is the last day of the offer. I'll just catch it.

They want to cheer me up now I have just clocked up another number and they think I might have an extra need to iron out wrinkles or tense muscles. I'm going for a facial. I don't often do this kind of thing and consider spending lots of money on what usually turns out to be an imperceptible 'improvement' a bit pointless, but today I happen to be free and it's only round the corner.

My therapist is a Felicity Kendal look-alike called Erika. She's from Hungary. By coincidence I am about to play a Hungarian hypnotherapist in a film. I start to tell her this, trying to make a bridge, but it becomes clear she doesn't speak much English. I feel a bit idiotic and shut up.

I lie back focusing on Erika's creamy, velvety strokes and I start to unfold and let go. Then letting go gets confused with loss. The tensions in my muscles are also banks of memories, stores of emotion. I don't want to be stroked into painful remembering . I tense up again. And then there is the music...

Nöel Coward was right: cheap music is very potent. How I hate these 'relaxing' soundscapes. Bland airy choirs, primitive pan pipes. If pink clouds could sing they would sound like this and it messes with my head. How can I go under when someone else's music is dictating the rhythm and landscape of my thoughts? An ooze of tears damps the lashes fringing my pursed eyes. I am floating into unhappy waters. When Peter was ill and after his death, I was regularly given a massage by a friend at her home. She too put on the looped tape of Clayderman and seagulls, and this is hitting the same spot. I could tell my friend to turn the music off. When you are known to be in mourning you can make demands. People understand and don't see it as rude. No questions asked and the instant switch into delicious silence.

But Erica knows her routine and doesn't know me. After quite a long internal battle I find the words: "Can we not have the music, please?" Erika slips out of the room. The controls are somewhere in the corridor. After several re-entries asking whether this lowered volume is "better?" she finally gets the idea that it is silence I want and that even subliminal whale music is a disturbance.

She works on in what I sense to be a bewildered silence. She isn't to know that her fingers are the touchstone of a luxurious sadness. She leaves the room for 10 minutes while the balm sinks into my skin. She will be booking her next client in and preparing my bill. During that time I actually fall asleep. Unheard of for me. When I wake to realise that fact a smile steals over my creamy face.

Erica comes back and wraps my face in towels. I feel like a snug papoose (or perhaps a corpse being lovingly prepared for her shroud). She is finishing a job, but to me it feels like love.

I shall come back again. It is only round the corner.

Toni Morrison | François Guillot/Getty Images

Maggie Smith, still from *Ladies In Lavender* (2004**)** | Georgia Oetker

Looking forward

I wish I was more like the Buddha, able to live in the present without aspirations or regrets. I have formed a lifetime's habit of looking at the day, the week, and the year ahead in terms of things to look forward to. The road is well over halfway travelled now so how will I frame my thoughts when there is very little road ahead to look forward to? Do we ever lose that habit of mind? I find part of my answer when I look at a few of the very old women I know. One tells me that she goes to the bus stop each morning and lets the first bus that comes along determine which museum or gallery she will visit that day. She keeps a full diary, looks forward to seeing the latest play or movie and has the latest novel by her bed. Another still teaches, which in a way implies a looking forward to the careers of her pupils even if she will never see them. Yet another has learnt what I cannot yet imagine learning, to sit still and enjoy the quietness. She once told me: "I like being old; it gives one time to think".

Irina Baronova | Chuck Burton/AP Press Association Images

Oksana Bryn teaches me to sing | Guy Paul 179

Susan Engel, with the cast of *Her Naked Skin* (2008) | Catherine Ashmore

From Here to Maturity Dance Company, a filmed rehearsal. From top to bottom, all by Georgia Oetker:
Jane East |
Jennifer Jackson and **Anne Dickie** |
Anne Dickie |
Lauren Potter, Simon Rice, Anne Dickie and **Jennifer Jackson** |

Above: **Camilla Smith** | Harriet Walter

Opposite: **Nobuko Somers (Hirose)** | Sophie Lambe

Living to be very old has a kind of cachet of its own.

Doris Lessing
(on being asked why she thought she had won the Nobel prize)

Georgia O'Keefe | Phillippe Halsman/Magnum

Old age is not an illness, it is a timeless ascent.
As power diminishes, we grow towards the light.

Mary Sarton

Mary Fedden | Lucinda Douglas-Menzies

Learn from the mistakes of others. You can't live long enough to make them all yourself.

Eleanor Roosevelt

Elsbeth Juda in her studio | Jill Kennington

It's not about future expectations but a deep satisfaction with the here and now, with yourself and your place in the world. It involves a degree of healthy self-esteem and a worldview that sets petty preoccupations against a wider canvas. It probably has little to do with money, though dire poverty will be its enemy. It depends on the falling away of all the things that blight our happiness when we're younger: ambition, competitiveness, stress, unfulfilled dreams and hopes.

Joan Bakewell

Above: **Mavis Mckelvey** | Katrin Talbot
Previous page both images: **Elisabeth Frink** | Jill Kennington

And now in old age I bud again,
After so many deaths I live and write;
I once more smell the dew and rain,
And relish versing.

George Herbert, *The Flower*

Colorado Woman | Katrin Talbot

For the past 20 years I have coped with old age by ignoring it – filling the house with friends and relations seeking a shoulder to cry on – and by following the advice of an elderly French noblewoman to "eat vegetables and take a lover".

Now the boyfriend is awaiting a triple bypass, too many vegetables upset me and I am tired of dispensing gin and sympathy – so I am going away. I shall travel during school holidays and take with me a teenage grandson who has not yet discovered girls.

Betty Matthews, The Times, 20 October 2003

There's special providence in the fall of a sparrow.
If it be now, 'tis not to come;
if it be not to come, it will be now;
if it be not now, yet it will come: the readiness is all.

William Shakespeare, Hamlet (Act V scene ii)

Postscript

We cannot reverse the ageing process. We can hide it and slow it down to a certain extent, but in the end we have to face it in ourselves. So why not try to befriend the inevitable? If we don't grow old, we die too young.

Opposite: **Jocelyn Ross** | Jill Kennington

Index of photographs
with credits and copyright information

Copyright information for texts: